RAIDERS OF THE LOST BARK

Illustrated by: Carl G. Moore
& Kevin Ahern

A SHOEBOX GREETINGS Book
(A tiny little division of Hallmark)

Andrews and McMeel • A Universal Press Syndicate Company • Kansas City

Other SHOEBOX GREETINGS Books from Andrews and McMeel
(A tiny little division of Hallmark)

The Mom Dictionary
Workin' Noon to Five
Don't Worry, Be Crabby!

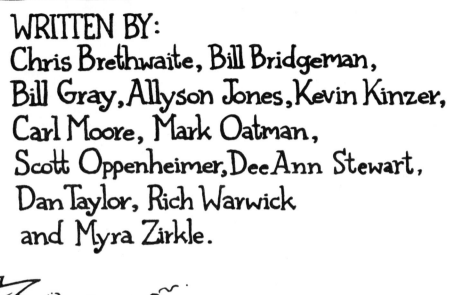

WRITTEN BY:
Chris Brethwaite, Bill Bridgeman,
Bill Gray, Allyson Jones, Kevin Kinzer,
Carl Moore, Mark Oatman,
Scott Oppenheimer, Dee Ann Stewart,
Dan Taylor, Rich Warwick
and Myra Zirkle.

CMOORE

ISBN: 0-8362-1731-4

Library of Congress Catalog Card Number: 93-71012

—————————— ATTENTION: SCHOOLS AND BUSINESSES ——————————

Andrews and McMeel books are available at quantity discounts for bulk purchase for educational, business, or sales promotional use. For information, please write to Special Sales Department, Andrews and McMeel, 4900 Main Street, Kansas City, Missouri 64112.

Dog Debates

5

Dog Practical Jokes

Dog Cooking Shows

For a while, Spot was content to beg at the table.
Then, one day, without warning...

Dog Analysis

DOG PERSONALS

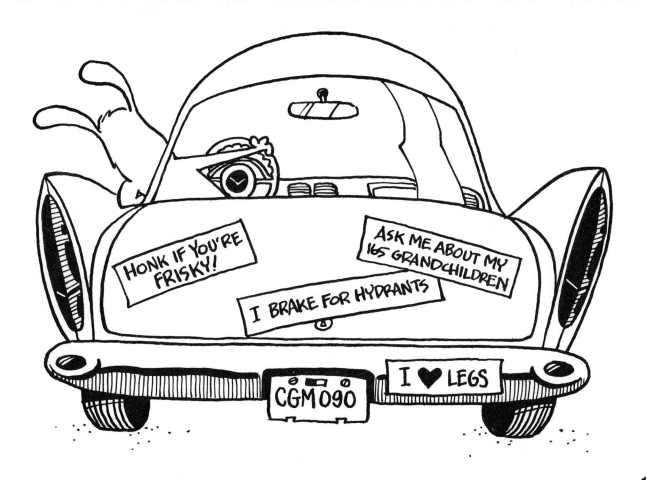

Why There Aren't Any Dog Restaurants

HOW THE WIENER DOG GOT ITS NAME

Pekingese Protests

17

Fifi Describes Her Blind Date

Every Day
Pierre Went
to the
Same Place
to Go to
the Bathroom

DADS OF THE DOG WORLD

Bosco Joins a Support Group
for Suckers of the Fake-the-Throw Gag

Lady MacBeth's Dog Chews Her Slippers
One Too Many Times

As the Result of a Misunderstanding, Ruff Fetches a Hick

IF DOGS HAD ANSWERING MACHINES

Rex Discovers That He Is, Indeed,
Barking Up the Wrong Tree

How the Bulldog Got Its Name

27

DOG FASHION MAGAZINES

Professor Davis Always Uses a Pointer

The Not-So-Great Dane

Another Sheepdog's Career Ruined
By Too Much Thinking

DOG COMICS

With His Owners on Vacation,
Spike Turns Entrepreneur

Dog Aerobics

AS THE DOG ASTRONAUTS GOT CLOSER TO THE MOON, THE HOWLING BECAME ALMOST UNBEARABLE

Shih Tzu Feeding Times

Why Dogs Shouldn't Become Orthopedic Surgeons

Four-Star Hotels for Dogs

41

Dog Bosses

Why Dogs Make Lousy Firemen

WILLARD SCOTTY

44

Why Dog Surprise Parties Don't Work

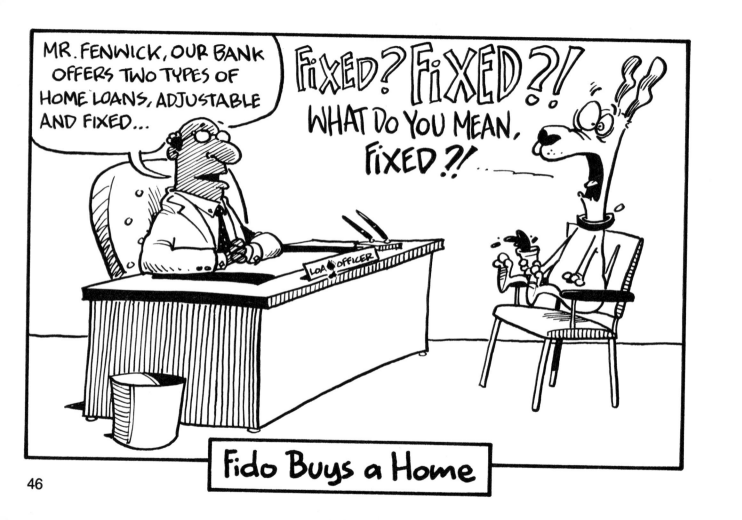

48 ALTHOUGH HE WAS A BERNARD, RUSTY WAS NO SAINT

Madge Learned the Hard Way Not to Wear
Her Bunny Slippers Jogging

50

Dog Romances

WHY DOG FORTUNE TELLERS HAVE IT EASY

One Thing Seemed Certain. Spotty Would Never Be Asked to Serve As Entertainment Chairperson Again

Dog Detectives

THROUGH AN UNFORTUNATE SCHEDULING MISHAP, PARTICIPANTS IN THE ANNUAL NEW YORK CITY DOG CONVENTION WERE TAKEN TO A PERFORMANCE OF "CATS"

Dog Attorneys

DOGS AT THE DRIVE-IN

Moms of the Dog World

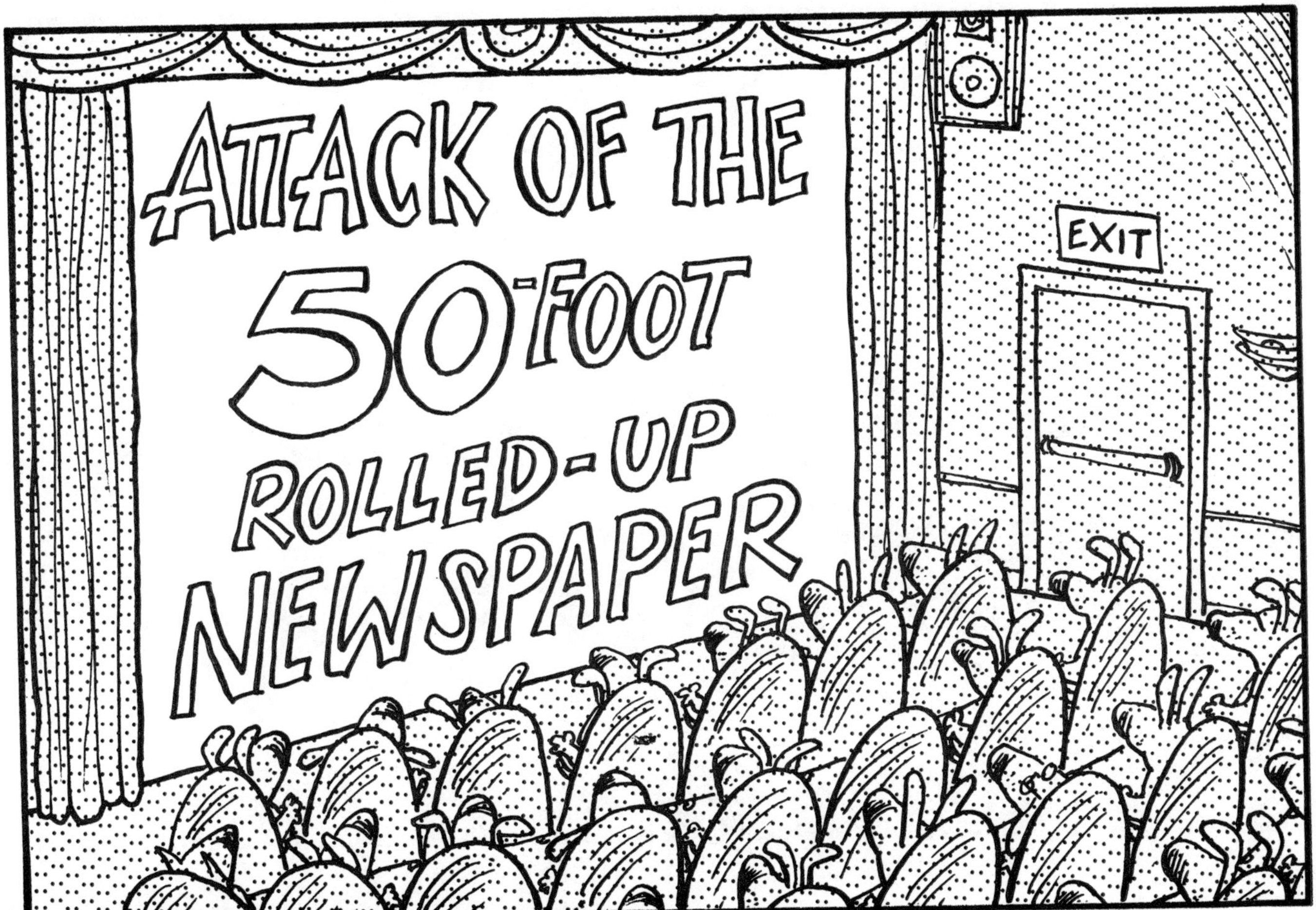
ATTACK OF THE
50-FOOT
ROLLED-UP
NEWSPAPER
EXIT

POLICE DOGS

Dog Peer Pressure

DOG RETIREMENT BANQUETS

Scotty Considered Himself a Scratch Golfer

69

Dog Commencement Speeches

Pepper Has an Attitude Problem

AN EMBARRASSING MOMENT AT THE DOG PHARMACY

73

When Dogs Dine Out

Lassie: The Later Years

DRIVER'S EDUCATION FOR DOGS

Dog Nightmares

The Indianapolis 500 for Dogs

DOG SERVICE STATIONS

Dog Rock Concerts

Riot at the Dog Prison

DOG TALK SHOWS

Weredogs

85

Why Dogs Make Lousy Baseball Players

Sparky's First Flight

AT THE DOG OPERA

Famous Dog Monuments

Why Dog Architects Have Such an Easy Job